A Dying Way of Life

A Dying Way of Life

Ben Dupree

WESTBOW·
PRESS
A DIVISION OF THOMAS NELSON
& ZONDERVAN

Scripture taken from the Holy Bible, NEW INTERNATIONAL VERSION®.
Copyright © 1973, 1978, 1984 by Biblica, Inc. All rights reserved worldwide.
Used by permission. NEW INTERNATIONAL VERSION® and NIV® are
registered trademarks of Biblica, Inc. Use of either trademark for the offering
of goods or services requires the prior written consent of Biblica US, Inc.

WestBow Press books may be ordered through booksellers or by contacting:

WestBow Press
A Division of Thomas Nelson & Zondervan
1663 Liberty Drive
Bloomington, IN 47403
www.westbowpress.com
1 (866) 928-1240

Because of the dynamic nature of the Internet, any web addresses or
links contained in this book may have changed since publication and
may no longer be valid. The views expressed in this work are solely those
of the author and do not necessarily reflect the views of the publisher,
and the publisher hereby disclaims any responsibility for them.

Any people depicted in stock imagery provided by Thinkstock are models,
and such images are being used for illustrative purposes only.
Certain stock imagery © Thinkstock.

ISBN: 978-1-4908-2827-5 (sc)
ISBN: 978-1-4908-2828-2 (e)

Library of Congress Control Number: 2014903677

Printed in the United States of America.

WestBow Press rev. date: 03/20/2014

For Kristin:
the woman found in Proverbs 31 longs for
the day she is as awesome as you.

Verse 31 says *Honor her for all her hands have done,
and let her works bring her praise at the city gate.*

Without you, this book would not exist.
I love you!

Contents

Introduction

The components of this book have been in the works for well over fifteen years. Mostly written in a deer stand and born out of the quietness it provided, I've found that I enjoy putting pen to paper and recording events, stories and lessons of my everyday life. I can recall reading a devotional whose name and author I've long forgotten that discussed Jesus' methods of teaching. It stated that we should mimic his teaching style by keeping it simple, keeping it short, being content to leave some things unsaid and forget about impressing others. I've tried to follow this advice in speaking and writing. The story or sermon ends because that's all there is. To go any further would be a waste of time for both of us. These stories follow that same pattern. Short and to the point.

However, before we get to the stories, I would like to present you with a rather lengthy list of my family members who have supported me and prayed for me, but most of all have provided material for me. Thank you Roy, Linda, Sam, Kim, Hannah, Madison, Rebekah, Dan, Debby, Rachel, John, Kristin, Reagan and Michael.

Enjoy, my friend. You are holding a dream come true.

A Lake Full of Memories

E arliest memories are special things. What is it about these everyday occurrences that causes them to latch on to one of our fledgling neurons and imprint that memory? Is there any correlation between that first memory and the passions and lifestyle that are to follow? I certainly hope so. You see, my earliest memory finds me on the deck at my parents' camp house on the shore of Black Lake. As if it were last week, I can recall propping my forehead on the hand rail that enclosed that deck, looking out at the lake and wondering when I was ever going to get the opportunity to start attending school. Since I got the opportunity to start school at the ripe old age of 4 and that camp house and its adjourning deck had fallen victim to flood waters in 1989 and even if that deck were still in existence, its handrail would catch me below the hip pocket, it's safe to say it wasn't last week but rather a long time ago.

I've always felt fortunate that my earliest memory involved something that is still precious to me today. I'm glad it wasn't of some irrelevant toy or household item. Rather, it was something that shaped who I am. Other fond memories include staring at my bright orange cork as I impatiently waited for it to wiggle over a bed of blue gills in May, watching a flock of buffleheads, mallards and canvas backs bank over our decoy spread in December, seeing my spinner bait suddenly jerk to the left as it passed a swell butt cypress and then halt and disappear simultaneously in June, giving my father a nervous nod for him to gun the engine as I tried to make my wobbly skis hydroplane for the hundredth time on the 4th of July, running the length of the dock and catapulting myself off the end with every intent of comparing my cannonball to that of my brothers on any random summer evening.

Not only did this lake offer abundant activities to a young boy growing up on its banks but I also credit it for keeping me out of trouble. During my college years, while most of my classmates were inhabiting bars and night clubs until the wee hours of the morning, I could be found slowly paddling down a bush line with a spotlight, a bucket of minnows and my yo-yos collecting the blue cat, white perch and occasional bass that dwell at the base of those trees. When given the choice to attend a bonfire kegger or to flip a rattletrap crank bait off the docks, the bass won every time. Even now I eagerly await my next opportunity to spend a weekend at my camp with my family. Words cannot express the joy I feel when my boys beat me to the dock with their cane poles and a can full of worms or the look on my eldest's face when he was presented with his very own bass fishing rig and tackle box.

My family and I have even been fortunate enough to draw alligator tags for our lake out of a public lottery. While catching a bass on a rod and reel or even an Opelousas catfish on a trotline is quite the thrill, nothing can compare to fighting a beast that is probably older than and is at least 3 feet longer than you. The fact I shared that experience multiple times with my parents, my sons, my brother, my niece and my wife made it special. The fact it all occurred on my home lake made it all the more memorable. Yes, first memories are special. I'm glad that mine occurred at the lake. I'm grateful for the millions that followed and I'm hopeful that it will be the location of my last.

There is an old sign hung near the door of
my camp. It bears a simple truth:

"Life is good at the lake."

That Nice Old Man

All cultures have stories and legends. Some are of heroic men or ungodly beasts. In my community such tales are common. Most tales are told about people of the past. One story is not really a "story" at all. The particular account I am about to share with you is about a man who lives among us and is spoken of like an old friend. My hunting buddy and I spoke of him frequently even though he was purely fictional—or so we thought until we met him.

The man of whom I speak was simply known as "that nice old man." You see, any time we were duck hunting in the rain, someone in the hunting party would say, "I sure wish that nice old man would bring us a cup of coffee" or "It would be great if that nice old man would pick up our decoys for us." On those cold spring nights when we had our catfish lines baited and it came time for the 2 a.m. run that seemed like such a good idea just a few hours before, we would remark how wonderful it would be if that nice old man would show up and run our hooks for us.

Requests for the nice old man's services evolved with the season. We wished he would help us drag a deer out of the woods in November only to wish for his motor boat to drag us in when our Evinrude outboard died on an April fishing trip. His generosity knew no bounds. Even though we knew he was not real and those catfish were not going to clean themselves, the simple thought of that nice old man always made us chuckle, and therefore made the task more bearable. Then came the day we met the legend himself.

My friend and I were driving up to a boat landing when we

noticed a boat trailer sticking out of the back of one of the parking spots. We launched our boat and when my friend returned from parking his truck, he asked, "Did you see that boat trailer?" I gave a positive reply. He grinned and said, "It's being pulled by a Cadillac!" We made several jokes about the town-and-country fisherman before we got underway.

Just a few bends in the creek later, we met this classy sportsman. He was an elderly gentleman who seemed content soaking his white perch jig. We exchanged pleasantries, wished him luck and departed. There was nothing strange or mystical about the old man so I soon forgot about the entire encounter.

We brushed our small duck blind on one of the numerous beaver ponds and headed home just before dark. When we reached the landing, my friend jumped out to get his truck. Once he reached his truck, he stopped. The purple fumes from the old Evinrude were making me rather light-headed. I idled the boat slowly back to where I had let him out to see what had him held up.

He was bent over beside the boat trailer. He motioned for me to kill the motor. When I stepped onto the bank, he pointed to our passenger-side boat trailer wheel. It had worked itself completely loose from the axle and was being held on by the remainder of the hubcap and a prayer. I was stunned! Then, I realized how lucky we were that he saw that wheel before we loaded up and took off down the highway.

"How in the world did you ever see that?" I asked. He opened his palm to reveal a small, tattered check stub. On the back there was a simple message. "Your back right trailer tire is about to fall off."

"It was on the windshield," he said as he studied our soon-to-be disaster. Then, I remembered. I spun around. The Cadillac and trailer were gone. "That sure was nice of him," I remarked.

"He probably just saved us an accident and a good chunk of money. If we had headed home without seeing this, we might have lost the whole rig."

"We were lucky to have made it down here with it like this," he replied. "Yep, that nice old man just saved us a heap of trouble." Then and there, we froze. That nice old man. He had helped us but in a way that we had never thought. Instead of cleaning fish, picking up decoys or any other things that could have been convenient, he saved us from causing damage to our boat trailer and truck and possible injury to ourselves. We drove home slowly and carefully, keeping a constant eye on that wobbling disc. We dropped off the trailer and went to look for the nice old man to thank him. We never did find him.

To this day, I have never seen the luxury car fisherman at any boat ramp again. He disappeared to resume his place among the legends. From this, I learned that guardian angels do not necessarily have wings. They can come to life from a story and take the form of a nice old man. God bless you sir, wherever you are.

The Floating Fire

⌢⁂⌢

When several teenage boys get together, the opportunities for folly are virtually endless. When these same boys go hunting together, their fathers try to talk them out of going but realize they went with their own friends when they were that age and eventually wish them luck, while their mothers pray for them and tell them to be careful.

These rituals were followed to perfection when I went duck hunting with several of my friends. We met at the boat landing with our guns, our fathers' shells, hand-me-down rubber waders that resembled a deep freeze on the inside, and a boat one of us sweet-talked out of his dad. We climbed in and off we went. We all sported our call lanyards like Olympic gold medals, only none of us were very good behind a double-reed. But that was all right. We were duck hunting. By ourselves. The fact that most of our waders leaked or that somebody forgot the decoys wasn't going to ruin this morning.

We pulled up next to a short finger of trees. My hunting partner, Alan Abels, and I jumped out. The water reached our waists. The driver gunned the engine when we were clear and the angry boil almost reached the top of our rubber britches. We fought sticky mud, deep holes and fallen limbs until we reached our desired trees. Like all of us expected, the sun rose and the ducks did not. Since we didn't have decoys, we decided to just stand next to the trees and hoped a duck would fly over. The next pair of boys was around the bend from us. We stood there, in freezing water, staring at a blue sky clear of clouds or ducks. I looked at Alan. He was beginning to shake some. When he spoke his voice was broken. When I tried to ask him what was wrong, my chattering jaw broke my words as well. It was cold. Finally I sputtered "Alan, are you ok?" "I'm freezing" came his vibrating reply.

Our misery was put on hold as we doubled up on a high wood duck. We eventually broke a wing and watched the drake sail some distance away. I looked at Alan and decided that I could be a good friend and go get the duck. So I began trudging through the silt. When I returned, Alan was gone. I hollered at him and his reply came from the tall grass several yards behind the trees. So again, I began to battle the sucking mud. Upon reaching the thicket I could see he had one boot up on a stump. "My waders started leaking," he chattered. I knew as cold as I was, being perfectly dry, he must be miserable. I looked at my clock. It was only 8:00 a.m. The pre-determined "let's-go home" point if the ducks weren't flying was 10:00.

I said, "It sure would be nice if we could build a fire." With land being over 100 yards away, we both knew a fire was out of the question. Then Alan turned to me, "We could burn the grass." "Good thinking," I said. We began to pile up beds of grass but to our disappointment even the tips of the grass were too damp to burn. "We need some gas to get this thing going," Alan muttered. But, the boat was around the bend and out of shouting distance.

Then Alan's eyes grew larger and he began to grin. "Gun powder," he said rather matter-of-factly. His look of excitement jumped to my face. "Get your pocket knife!" he ordered as he retrieved some rusty Federal steel shot shells from his pocket. He began to whittle on his shells and soon we had a small mound of black powder on a layer of grass floating on the muddy water. "Get some more grass ready," I said. When we had the grass in hand we put it on top of the first layer with a thin finger of the powder running away from the mound. I lit the powder peninsula and Alan dropped the remainder of the grass. The sudden surge of fire brought the tips of the weeds to a smolder. Soon, small yellow flames were leaping out of the edges of the grass pile. When Alan saw the flames he added another helping of powder followed by grass. The fire, which was floating in about a foot of water, thrived. We sat down on some stumps and enjoyed the unusual luxury.

When our friends returned to pick us up they were shaking. Their ears and cheeks were red from the cold and one of the boys was down to his t-shirt thanks to a submerged limb that caused him to do a face-first in the water. They rounded the bend and there we were, sitting on stumps just above the water's surface talking, laughing and enjoying a nice raging fire, one that could be moved if we were getting hot or cold.

The looks on their faces showed bewilderment. However, to this day, I don't know which shocked them more, the floating fire or the fact that the wood duck floating in the orange reflection was the only duck of the morning.

For Alan,

"Here's to the sunny slopes of long ago."

-Augustus McCrea

The Duck Blind Schizophrenic

Our society has never failed to have its elite search out and document those things which intrigue us. Whether these things are photographs of Bigfoot or a cure for cancer, our scholars generate volume after volume of facts, figures and assumptions to keep us informed. It is with deepest regrets that I tell you we have failed.

I have stumbled across a phenomenon of epic proportions and not one drop of ink has been applied in documentation. This enigma exists throughout the world in the duck blinds, swamps and marshes. These places have strange powers over sane men and are capable of altering their psyche. So I suppose we can call this Volume I of the duck blind schizophrenic.

I believe I am well-qualified to write about this since I've witnessed these happenings first hand and also been affected by them. For this documentation, I will use my own duck blind and hunting party as the basis. I usually duck hunt with several people. My hunting party consists of anywhere between 2-6 hunters, mostly relatives. When I first noticed this sickness I thought it was unique unto my family. Since that time I have had the opportunity to hunt with several different individuals from outside my extended kinship. Through these hunts, I have learned that all hunters are prone to developing this horrid disease.

Hunters who become affected will take on an alter-ego between the duck blind and their pick-ups. Allow me to explain, again using myself and my family as examples. When a group of ducks sweeps over our spread, as many as 18 shots can be fired. So as you can imagine it can be rather difficult to determine who killed what.

When the gun fire dies down all of us began to vocalize what each hunter thinks he killed. Now to listen to us talk there should be about 15 dead ducks in or around our spread. However the final tally of those floating remains in the single digits.

Now the arguments begin. Hunters bicker over who killed what. Sayings such as "I know I killed 2 ducks," and "All I'm saying is the 3 I shot at folded" run rampant. They (excuse me…We) will spend several minutes fighting like 1st graders over a toy until another doomed flock takes our minds off the argument.

Then when these ducks fall the process repeats itself. We'll fight until it is time to go home. We reach the lake's edge, unload our guns, shells and of course the disputed ducks. It is here and only here that the alter-ego of all duck hunters makes itself known. All the ducks are piled on a tailgate and the argument subsides for a brief moment. Somebody will say "I guess all these ducks are yours." Then comes the reply, "No you said you killed them. You take them." "No you were right, I missed." "Aw I was just joking. You're a better shot than I am. Go ahead and take them." "You know the more I thought about it the more I think I pulled off. I'm pretty sure you killed them."

To the non-hunter this conversation would be jaw-dropping to witness. Here are these grown men building each other up with compliments that just moments ago were entangled in an argument so deeply disputed that not even their wives were considered off-limits. As you may have figured out we all love to duck hunt. It's the cleaning of the duck that we try to avoid.

Now the facts have been presented. They come from first-hand documentation of an eye witness. Now it is up to you, America, to draw your own conclusions. Do some church-going, honest men switch personalities? Does a duck really hold such power over its pursuers? Does the swamp make men change?

Further research may be required.

The Flight

M y father stepped into my room and gave his usual hunting season greeting. "Boy, get up. I'm not coming in here again." He flicked on the lamp as he left the room. When I gained enough consciousness and heard the sound of a warm November rain, I stumbled out of the bed into the living room. I reached for my pile of clothes on the kitchen table that I had laid out the night before. Then the contemplation began. The temperature was in the mid-70s. We had not had good luck in the blind all week, and it was pouring rain. My hesitation caught my father's attention. He knew what I was thinking. "Go back to bed, son." I didn't even try to complain.

As I was drifting off I heard my father laugh to my brother as he opened the door, "He's probably the smartest one of the bunch." The rain eased the guilt of missing a hunt and soon I was in that duck blind I visited every night where the ducks were plentiful. This dream hunt was cut short by the ringing of a phone. Through the static I recognized the voice of my oldest brother on his cell phone. "Get dressed and get down here." When I asked why, the line was dead.

Confusion set in. I threw on a slicker, grabbed my gun and left. After battling a misting rain and slick muddy roads, I arrived at the boat landing. I called for them on my 2-way radio and I soon heard the boat putting my way. My father and brother picked me up and they were all smiles. When we reached the blind I was speechless. About 200 mallards flushed out of our spread. As we rushed into the blind, I noticed I was the only one with a gun. "What's the deal?" I asked. My brother just grinned.

They had gotten their limit! I was the only shooter on the biggest flight I had ever seen. Flight days are missed by many people due to not being there when the ducks come. Flights are unforeseen and unpredictable; they just happen. Other nearby blinds were empty. The rain and no ducks had gotten the better of them. The ducks just kept coming. I remember seeing ducks on the water, groups trying to sit down, hundreds above them very intent on our spread and new ducks still arriving. We would have groups of 200 trying to light all at once. At one time I let one group get too close and I didn't have a clean shot. I shot into a wad of green heads and completely missed. The birds were so thick that my pattern found a grey duck on the edge of our spread. My poor shooting allowed me to enjoy this miracle a while longer. When I had my six floating, we just sat and watched. Shortly, the flight ended.

I have not seen anything like this before and I consider myself lucky to have seen it in my life. That night as I lay down, I visited that same duck blind with very vivid details. To think I almost slept through the chance of a lifetime.

Wood Glue, Bubble Gum
and other Cover-Ups

While you were growing up, were you ever "bad"? Was there a time or activity that you desperately tried to keep away from the rude gaze of the public? Were your cover-up tactics successful? Allow me to tell you of a time where mine were not.

I come from a rather large family. I am the youngest of three boys and we all get together at my parents' house every Sunday for dinner. So, as you can imagine it can make for a crowded house and cluttered driveway. One Sunday, while the rest of the family was inside, I was backing out my mother's car from their carport. While doing so, I was keeping a careful eye on my sister-in-law's car bumper as I tried to navigate past it. Once I cleared her vehicle, I leaned as far as I could forward to make sure I didn't collide with another vehicle as I began to now move forward. I was so intent on the passenger side fender, I did not notice that one of the numerous pine trees in my parents' yard had grown somewhat audacious and had jumped right in front of my mother's car. The tree clipped the edge of the bumper. When I got out to make sure no one heard the collision and to check for damage, I noticed a chunk of pine bark was now missing from this fearless tree. For anyone who has ever gazed upon a freshly skinned pine tree, you know the exposed wood shines like a new penny. I knew I was busted.

After checking on the car and seeing no real damage, I leaned down to inspect the scarred tree. As I touched the bare wood, I realized it was sticky with sap. Then, I had an idea. I began to replace the bark using this natural adhesive. However, this first attempt was met with failure as the bark quickly fell back to the earth. But, I was not going down without a fight. After a quick glance around to make sure I was still undetected, I ran around the house to my father's shed and retrieved the wood glue. By the time I was done, that bark was replaced so beautifully it would've made Mother Nature jealous. As I closed my eyes that night, I can recall smirking "I have got it made! They'll never find out." It was as if the Almighty laughingly said, "Wanna bet?" It rained that night and the wood glue didn't have the opportunity to set up. My mother was enjoying her morning coffee on the front porch when a funny looking spot on a pine tree caught her eye. One tap with the toe of her slipper and my masterpiece crumbled to the ground. The words of Isaiah 3:9, "*The look on their faces testifies against them,*" come to mind as I recall my mother entering my room that morning inquiring about the wood glue on the tree. Turns out, I'm not that good at covering up mistakes. As I learned that morning, I was not nearly as gifted as my father was at it.

Once he found out about my failed attempt, he told me of a cover-up from his own childhood that was wildly successful. He and my uncle grew up in a time when the federal government did not regulate what went into fireworks. They heard a rumor that a true "cherry bomb" would explode even under water. Well, the only water they had readily available in the yard was a steel bucket they had found after the military had conducted maneuvers in the area and that my grandfather had used to water his cows. They lit the fuse, dropped the bomb and stepped away to see if the rumor was proven to be correct. What they weren't told was that a cherry bomb will go off under water with the same impressive force as on dry ground. The explosion split my grandfather's favored watering bucket right down the side. Knowing their rears were as good as red if my grandfather discovered his ruined receptacle, they got to work. They each grabbed a side of that cracked bucket and pushed until they got the sides to touch. They then proceeded to melt a rubber inner tube to fill the void. After that, they chewed several packs of bubble gum and smeared that inside the bucket to create a smooth surface. They put the finishing touches on their cover-up by spray painting the bubble gum silver. As you can imagine, at the conclusion of this story, I was in shock and fighting back the urge to take notes. However, the story left me with one unanswered question. "Daddy, how did you and Uncle Johnny keep Papaw from seeing that strip of melted rubber running down the side of the bucket?" He replied, "Son, we turned that crack to the post and kept that watering bucket filled religiously for the next 20 years."

As I look back on my family's follies, I'm reminded of another great cover up that we find in scripture. Second Samuel 11:1-5 says, *"In the spring, at the time when kings go off to war, David sent Joab out with the king's men and the whole Israelite army. They destroyed the Ammonites and besieged Rabbah. But David remained in Jerusalem.² One evening David got up from his bed and walked around on the roof of the palace. From the roof he saw a woman bathing. The woman was very beautiful, ³ and David sent someone to find out about her. The man said, "She is Bathsheba, the daughter of Eliam and the wife of Uriah the Hittite." ⁴ Then David sent messengers to get her. She came to him, and he slept with her. (Now she was purifying herself from her monthly uncleanness.) Then she went back home. ⁵ The woman conceived and sent word to David, saying, "I am pregnant."*

Back in those days, kings and armies planted their crops in the spring, went away for battle during the fair-weathered summer and returned for the harvest in the fall. Here, we witness David's first mistake. He simply rolled out of bed, looked at his responsibility to that day, and thought to himself "Nah, I just don't feel like going to work today." How many of us have ever had one of those mornings? Statements like "Well, with a cold front moving in, the deer are liable to be stirring in the morning." or "Tomorrow would be a great morning to hit the ol' fishing hole," may sound a bit more familiar. Pretty harmless, right? I mean, we've all done it. But, by his avoiding his responsibility, he was faced with and gave in to a temptation to which he should have never been exposed. Verses 14-17 tell us, *"In the morning David wrote a letter to Joab and sent it with Uriah. 15 In it he wrote, "Put Uriah out in front where the fighting is fiercest. Then withdraw from him so he will be struck down and die."16 So while Joab had the city under siege, he put Uriah at a place where he knew the strongest defenders were. 17 When the men of the city came out and fought against Joab, some of the men in David's army fell; moreover, Uriah the Hittite died."* So, we see that in a short period of time, he went from simply ignoring his responsibility to committing adultery to facilitating the death of a man in order to cover up his own sin.

David had built up a false sense of security that he had hid his sin. However, through the prophet Nathan, he learns that he hasn't hid anything from the Almighty. As we learn from David, all sin has consequences and he had to endure a parent's worst nightmare. But, let's stop and ask ourselves "Could David ever earn God's love again? Can we?" The answer may shock you because it's a resounding "No!" No, he could not and we cannot. But, that did not stop God from giving it freely to David and offering it freely to us. We can experience forgiveness and freedom of sin by doing exactly what David did, and admitting our sin is nothing short of a slap in the face of God.

In the end, our cover-ups are about as dependable as wood glue and bubble gum.

A Water-Leak Baptism

I like dogs. Always have. My father has always raised beagles and I truly believe the human heart has yet to see a relationship as pure and trusting as that of a young boy and his first puppy. However, at the outset of this tale, I must inform you that there was an occasion where I was not very fond of one canine in particular. My eldest brother and his family raise Labrador retrievers--sweet, loyal animals that take full advantage of the fact that my brother lives on Black Lake.

They had a young female come in heat and they decided now was not the ideal time to have to have another crop of puppies. So they locked her up to prevent her from being bred. The resident lady's man Labrador did not take kindly to his night life being tampered with and he took out his frustration on everything in sight. He would howl all night. He would destroy a child's toy left in the yard. Then he found the water hose. The testosterone-possessed animal chewed, gnawed, shredded and eventually began to use his jaws to yank on said water hose. Now let me explain something here. Lakefront property has a tendency to become underwater property after long periods of rainfall. That is what had happened, and the hose was attached to a faucet, controlled by a valve, which was now about 3 feet under the lake. Apparently, the dog really missed his female companion because he yanked with enough force to snap the faucet the stress-relieving hose was attached to right off its PVC stem. A geyser ensued.

The next morning my father noticed the fountain in my brother's yard, and since my brother was at work and I was enjoying one of my off days from college, I was chosen as my father's aide.

It was a cold spring day and the rains had swollen the lake far beyond its boundaries. So, needless to say, when my father burst into my room and ordered me to put on my waders, he obtained my undivided attention as well as elevating my interest. He hurried down the hall, shouting out a mixture of orders and explanations. "Sam has a water leak. Meet me over there." I realized at this point that any hopes I had of this being a quick fix or even an easy task followed my frustrated father right out the door.

Sam had a water leak. We had to shut his water off at the shut-off valve. The valve is in Sam's front yard. The lake is up and Sam's front yard is now approximately three and a half feet under the water. Finding the valve would be difficult. The task of actually shutting off the valve, I'd yet to ponder. I can recall standing at the water's edge, hands tucked firmly inside the pockets of my waders, trying to squeeze further down into my hooded sweatshirt and away from the brisk breeze. Seeing the fountain off to my left, my brother's house out front, I watched my father emerge from his own house to my right. But something was missing. By "something" I mean my father's coat, waders and even shoes. All he had on was a pair of thin, gray coveralls. Before I could ask just what exactly he had on his mind, he gave me more orders, "The valve is behind that tree. I think. We've got to find it." I didn't question or complain. I simply obeyed.

I now believe that trying to locate and identify something with your neoprene-clad feet under murky lake water should be an Olympic event. After several false alarms (i.e. sticks, holes, toys the demon dog didn't find, etc.), I located the box containing the valve in water well above my waist. When I announced my find to my not-so-patiently waiting father, he charged into the chilly waters. As he waded in, my father's voice rose right along with the water level on his body. By the time he reached me, he could have qualified for the soprano section in the choir.

Then the torture began, at least for him. He took a knee and started his initial attempt to reach the valve. The problem was that the valve rested at the bottom of a plastic box that reached an additional foot into the earth. I can still see him--the muddy water reaching his beard, his body beginning to tremble, as he rose to his feet in disgust, shaking his head violently. The rest of his body was now shaking on its own. I felt bad. Here was my father, soaked and vibrating after kneeling in nippy lake water and there I was, warm and dry with my only contribution being locating the sunken valve. I offered to take his place but he would hear nothing of it. Through muttering lips, he announced Phase II of his plan. "Son, I'm going to have to go under." This statement was followed by an awkward silence on my part.

As he stared at his fate, all I could manage was a stumbling "uh...OK." The plan was simple. I was to put my foot in the hole, my father was to follow my leg to the box, reach for the valve and presto, I could go back to bed. Again, he took a knee as I ran my foot into the box. "You ready?" I asked as I placed a hand on his shoulder. He gave a jerky nod and down he went. Now my father is a big man. So when he went out of sight and his long legs kicked to pin him to the bottom, he was making quite the commotion. Mud boiled around as I tried to steady myself against his thrashing. The number of seconds that had passed coupled with the fact the spout was still flowing began to cause concern. I could still feel him flouncing about but I began to worry.

What if his sleeve was ensnared on the valve? What if he couldn't resurface? I began to yell into the water, "Have you found it yet?" Boiling, muddy, lake water was the only reply. It was at this juncture, I realized we were not alone, nor had we been for some time. Movement from the houses caught my eye. There, with her truck door open wide, and taking several cautious steps towards the water, was the meter reader. For those of you who've never experienced life in a rural setting, a meter reader is usually an older post-retirement-age person who makes monthly rounds to record the usage on various utilities for billing purposes. There she stood, her mouth as open as her truck door, notebook fallen to her side and eyes as big as coffee cups. I don't know how long the dear lady had witnessed this spectacle, but I didn't get the chance to ask. As soon as she became aware she had been detected, she sprinted back to her truck and away she went.

About this time, my father resurfaced, mumbling unintelligible syllables. Anxiously, I looked toward the gusher. Still gushing. Perhaps it takes a few seconds for the water line to be depleted. No such luck. I looked down at my father. He wiped the dirty water away from his face with a trembling hand as he stayed in a kneeling position. When he attempted to speak his voice was weaker, broken. As the lake-bottom mud dripped out of his beard, he reached up and grabbed my arm as he admitted, "Can't... can't reach." I wrapped my arm around his chest determined this time to lift him out of that hypothermia-inducing water. I was his son. I was younger and felt I should save him from this icy torment. "Get up and go inside. Get in the shower. I'll finish this." With eyes closed, he shook his head and managed to sputter "No...no, I'll...I'll do it." He halted my next wave of protest with a raised hand. He looked at me and with a trembling voice said, "Son, I'm going to need you to hold me under." Words fail in moments such as these.

My father had just asked me to hold him under water. During my silence, he began to slowly explain his plan. I was to grab him by the collar and plunge him into the depths while he followed my leg back to the box. Then as he held himself down by clinging to that leg, I was to plant my other foot between his shoulder blades and pin him to the bottom, thereby freeing his arms up to complete the task at hand. When it was completed, he was to tap me on the leg and I would let him up. Simple, right? I mean who has never been asked to drown their father?

So there we were in murky water, waist-deep on me, chin-deep on my father. I grabbed a handful of his collar as he muttered "Jesus!" out of frustration. I asked him if he was ready. With his eyes closed and face upturned, he nodded yes. Down he went. He was still thrashing about and I began to wonder if I was confusing his movements for the "I'm done, let me up" tap I was expecting. So I began to repeatedly shout "Have you found it yet?" into the water to the man whose collar I had driven toward the bottom. After about my third shout, I noticed that the meter reader had returned with reinforcements.

She had returned with three friends. While I observed their actions, it dawned upon me what they thought they were witnessing. Two of them stood near the truck and were already on the second verse of "Amazing Grace." A third stood closer to the water, hands raised, anointing the entire situation in prayer. The meter reader, after my third shout into the depths, yelled at me waving her Bible in her hand. "Sonny, if he ain't found Jesus by now, let him up!" Before I could explain, we all noticed the "fount-of-many-blessings" die. I felt the tap and brought my father back up.

I believe the ladies were satisfied with our activities and quickly vacated the premises. I immediately ordered my father to go straight to the shower and then have a cup of coffee. As for me, I located and chained that male lab before he started a revival on the lake's edge.

With the exception of one chilly spring
morning, a finer animal has yet to exist.

Claude

R.I.P

1990-2005

The Silent Victory

Back in the early parts of the 20th century, small towns dotted the wooded countryside of north Louisiana. Each of the communities had its own small school which spanned kindergarten to high school. Town would rise against town every weekend for the basketball competitions that were held in barn-like gymnasiums. Older men in the communities can still remember very vivid facts of their time on the hard-wood courts. Besides the church house, the gym would be the main place the townspeople would congregate.

Now times have changed. Several of the smaller schools have been closed and the rural students have been shipped off to university-like campuses. When these small schools died, many times the town would follow suit. One such town lost its high school but was able to keep its elementary school. Now almost every high school in this parish has been shut down and a few very large, heavily-populated high schools have been built. Recently a proposal was made to build an enormous elementary school right next to one of these high schools. If this school were to be built, the small-town elementary school would inevitably fold. Support for this new school came from everywhere. On the day the proposal was brought to a vote, those who were in favor of the new school were out in full force gathering up votes. Barbeque stands were set up as near to voting booths as the law would allow and the people flocked to the polls. Talk of a huge victory party danced around the confident bunch. Buses were rented to pick up voters and all of them were given instructions on how to vote. Several supporters laughed about how the construction crew could go ahead and break ground. But somewhere under the festive scramble stood a small town determined to survive.

Without fanfare, the citizens converged on the voting booths. When the polls closed, the confidence of those who wanted the new school soared; however, that confidence was short-lived. When the results were revealed, they showed a miracle—a victory for the small school. As the sure-to-be stunned winners quietly left with no words to say, a town celebrated, not with a huge party or feast nor with fireworks or rallies. They celebrated this victory silently. They simply went to bed with the reassurance that their town and school would be there in the morning and many mornings to come.

Long live Goldonna School and her beloved Wildcats.

27/17!

I'd Like to Meet Him

We all have people we would like to meet. Most likely they are people we have only seen from afar. Those people probably have represented us, entertained us or inspired us in one way or another. For example I would like to have the opportunity to shake Billy Graham's hand and sit down and talk with George W. Bush. But there is one man I would like to meet even though I have no idea who he is, what he does for a living, or where he is from. All I know about him is that he is a good man and that he hunts ducks on Black Lake. Now for the story.

A buddy and I grew frustrated with all the warm December weather and lack of ducks. We wanted to do something to actually put some meat on the table. So we got to thinking. In the warm spring time of the year the blue cats, white perch and the occasional bass gather in the shallow waters around the islands of Black Lake. So we decided that just like in the spring we would grab our auto-fishers (affectionately known as yo-yos) and hit the lake. We reached one of our favorite islands known as the Sand Bar and figured it looked as good as any. So we began to encircle this group of trees.

When we reached the far end of the sandbar, we saw something that got us to thinking. There, anchored to some trees, was a duck blind. Now technically it *was* duck season. But you could have counted all the shots we heard on the lake in the past month without having to take your shoes off. Since the forecast showed the following morning to be still, clear and warm, we thought that surely the owner of the blind would find something better to do than come out here and stare at an empty blue sky.

We kept right on hanging those shiny yo-yos all around his blind. We were so confident that the man would not show up that we even took advantage of a low limb that had been used to brush the duck blind's entrance. We finished circling the island and left to go circle another one. We ran those hooks all night with some pretty good success. Then the following morning my father met us at the boat pool. He had been out to run his trotline. He asked us if we had the yo-yos around the Sand Bar. We said yes figuring he saw a huge number of catfish heads sticking out of the water. He asked us if we noticed the duck blind on the far end of it. It was then that we started to realize something was amiss.

He said, "Boys, you're not going to believe this but it has a Robo in front of it." (A Robo-duck is a spinning-winged decoy that runs off of batteries and is never left out all night). My friend and I looked down and then at each other. "Really?" my friend said with a my-God-I-hope-you're-joking look on his face. My father just nodded. Then he said, "The whole Sand Bar is shining like a bunch of mirrors." So we figured it was time to face the music.

We loaded up and drove to the sandbar all ready to apologize to the man who was sure not to kill any ducks with dozens of bright, reflective discs all around his blind. But thankfully when we got there he was already gone. We started to take our fish and pick up our yo-yos, carefully counting to see if the frustrated hunter did away with any. We were sure that all we would find of that yo-yo, which was tied to the entrance to his blind, was a frazzled string. But we were wrong. The yo-yo was not even tied to the limb on the blind. The hunter moved it to a limb right next to it. Not only was he nice enough to move the yo-yo, but he also left a two pound blue cat hanging on it.

So, mister, I would imagine that men of your character and forgiveness are few and far between. I'd like to say that I am truly sorry and thank you. Maybe one day we'll meet.

Duck Calls and Parking Lots

W e've all had days where things just went right. A basketball
player might have a day where all he had to do was toss
the ball in the vicinity of the goal and swish! Nothing but net.
A baseball player may have a batting practice where he feels as
though he could produce solid line-drives blindfolded. A bass
fisherman could have an outing where he could place his spinner
bait in a coffee cup fifty yards away. It is during these times, I
believe the good Lord merely takes away our ability to screw up.
Same as you, I've had a precious few of those days, but I'd like to
tell you about one such day that stands head and shoulders in my
memory above them all.

I was in college majoring in education. It was the fall semester
and I was enrolled in a "teaching methods class," which is pretty
much the boot camp of the education field. You're assigned to
a teacher and a class. You must observe hours and hours of the
teacher instructing his pupils, conduct class profiles (gender, race,
socio-economic group, etc.), monitor student engagement, and
note what teaching strategies seemed to have the desired effect.
Then you must prepare for your own time in front of the students
by creating lesson plans that are usually the length of the Old
Testament, that must record every material needed, every activity
conducted and every syllable uttered during the lesson. Then these
proposed plans are handed over to the teacher to be crucified.

I was blessed to have been assigned to one of the greatest
teachers I've ever met. His name was Mr. Phillip McClung. As I
observed his eighth-grade classroom with its well-oiled routines
and his approachable, caring demeanor toward the child that

couldn't wait for his class to begin, I knew what I wanted my own classroom to feel like. Most observations were about as exhilarating as watching turtles race, but I found myself strangely disappointed when my required hours were fulfilled in Mr. McClung's room. It was now time for him to hand the reins over to me and for him to grade *my* performance. He immediately noticed and complimented me on my passion for story-telling. He also perceived and chastised my tendency to fly by the seat of my pants instead of following the lesson.

The day came for my final lesson with Mr. McClung and "our" students. My paperwork referred to it as an "Enrichment" lesson which had been explained to me as a lesson on a topic that I personally knew a great deal about but with which the children were not familiar. As long as it fit into these parameters, anything went. So that got me to thinking. Upon what topic could an ol' country boy educate a bunch of city kids?

Since I would imagine the administration would frown upon me gutting a deer or filleting a white perch on school property, I settled on the sport of duck hunting. My lesson included decoys, images of waterfowl native to the great state of Louisiana, revenue generated by hunters, species identification, etc. I even pulled up a website that was dedicated to the sport of water fowling which at the time, I served as a field editor. The students had the opportunity to see my picture and read my articles. I could tell that even Mr. McClung was impressed. My "A" was so close, I could taste it. All that was left was a brief demonstration with the duck calls and my time in methods was done.

We decided to take the calling seminar outside so as to not disturb the other classes. This school sat on the edge of Northwestern State University facing a busy intersection that led to the interstate as well as being home to banks, fast food restaurants, condo apartments and a supermarket. As the students gathered outside, I explained what a duck call was, what it can be made of and how to use it. I explained and demonstrated the various calls of different species and genders. I explained what different calls meant and how they were used. I went through the attention-getting high ball of a mallard hen and the raspy hum of a mallard drake. Then, I finished my presentation with the contented 3-quack series of a laid-back female.

When I was done, I dropped the call from my mouth and said to the not-so-interested kids "and that will usually bring them in." Mr. McClung, who had been listening to my display with great intensity, sprang to the front of the class, gazed over their heads and jokingly said, "Well, I don't see any!" At that exact moment, a wide-eyed young lady in the front row pointed over our heads and said, "Mr. McClung! Look!" We spun around and there was a group of about fifteen ducks low enough to tell they were pintails. As they banked back over the school building and left the premises via the wind above the supermarket, my eyes fell back to the class. When the ducks were out of sight, teacher and students alike looked at me with mouths agape. Slowly, I returned the lanyard to my neck, met their disbelieving gaze and, while desperately trying to keep a straight face, stated, "And that, boys and girls, is how it's done. Questions?"

With the class rendered speechless, I dismissed them back to the room. Mr. McClung approached, slapped me on the back as he stared at the ground and stated slightly above a whisper, "I think you're getting an A."

For Mr. Phillip McClung, who is
everything a teacher should be.

Worth Passing On

Growing up, I always wanted to be a teacher. I loved history and loved being in front of people so the field of education seemed to fit. Plus, the large breaks during hunting season and summer always came in handy. I feel that I will always be a teacher, no matter how many times my situations or subject matter may change.

Having graduated from college with a bachelor's degree in Secondary Education of Social Sciences and a Master's degree in Educational Leadership and having spent thus far 10 years in the classroom, I've had the opportunity to hear many lectures and participate in numerous workshops and seminars. All of these events had the sole purpose of making me a better teacher, a better-equipped educator, if you will. Although some of these speakers were quite good and I'm sure I'll see the importance of those workshops down the road, I've come to the realization that they all failed. Because of them, I may be better equipped to interpret a curriculum and I may be more knowledgeable about the latest technology, but I have learned nothing about what makes a teacher great. None of them have taught me who I am or where I came from or what my students can take away from *me* instead of the textbook.

The best lecture I've ever sat through, the most informed historian about events, both local and overseas, that I have ever met, has been my adopted grandfather Mr. Lloyd "Pete" Stewart. As I sat there in his living room, I've learned about family members I never had the opportunity to meet. I've heard war stories from the invasion of southern France. I've been brought back over the decades to truly see where and who I came from. These stories are lessons I feel I must pass on to my own children and students. From this "Papaw," I've learned about my biological grandfathers and what they were like before old age altered their minds and bodies. I've listened to hunting and fishing stories that took place in the same creeks and swamps I still frequent today. Through him, I can see how my small hometown of Goldonna, Louisiana, has changed over the years

The lessons that he taught me are priceless. He never once showed me how to use technology in my classroom nor did he ever display the most current method of creating lesson plans. But my classroom is more alive because of the history that he passed on to me. My students will hopefully benefit from his lively stories that I have passed on to them.

My prayer is that my students will not only learn to appreciate history, whether it be global or local, but that they will be better persons and live their lives in such a way that they might leave a legacy worth passing on. From Papaw Pete I found the old saying is true: "The best classroom in the world is at the feet of the elderly."

Lloyd "Pete" Stewart

September 16, 1923 - January 15, 2005

This Too Shall Pass

◯—m—◯

M y grandmother, Gertrude Dupree, was born in 1905. I
dearly cherished the time spent with her and the feeling
seemed mutual. Out of five grandsons, I was her youngest and
I was spoiled. After school, I would always walk to her house,
open the door and announce, "Hey, Mamaw!" I can still see
her peeking from around the corner out of the kitchen as she
hollered back, "Hey, Baby!" I would sit on her old pink couch
with great anticipation of spending time with her and listening to
tales from days gone past, as I snacked on the seemingly endless
pile of goodies she kept for me. Oh, how the tales did come!
This woman witnessed so many things in her life. To put it in
perspective, when she was born there were Civil War veterans still
alive. She lived through two world wars and watched her husband
leave to fight for the U.S. Navy in the latter of the two. She
saw the implementation of such things as indoor plumbing, the
automobile and television and the demise of the likes of the horse
and buggy, segregation and the railroad that once ran through
our small town.

One such day as I sat on her couch, she asked me how my
day had gone. I can recall complaining about some particular
injustice that had occurred at school that day. The crime itself
has become irrelevant to my memory. It was her response that
stood out to me. She looked at me with certainty in her blue
eyes and said, "Child, this too shall pass." She said it, not with
hope, but with confidence. Her many years on this earth had
apparently taught her this binding truth. Her look literally
snatched away all fear about the future. This difficult time, and

all others to come for that matter, will eventually pass. I left her couch that day feeling better knowing whatever deeply political scandal had upset this fourth grader's universe would not last forever.

However, there was a difficult day yet to come. It was October 10, 1995. On that day, I found myself by her bedside, holding her hand as she entered glory. I can still recall that same look of certainty as she looked at me for the last time and although she did not speak, I could hear the words echo, "Child, this too shall pass." That day and the pain it brought did eventually pass but missing her has yet to cease. I felt strangely honored that out off all the things she saw while on this earth, the last of them was me.

Since then, I've graduated high school and college, begun my career as a teacher, met the woman of my dreams, married her and settled down. During these years, I've also encountered multiple other days where I would grit my teeth with the frustration that comes with being a teacher and remind myself of her words of wisdom: "This too shall pass."

One such day occurred and I came home to my young wife in a frump of a mood. As she and I sat down to supper, she asked me what was on my mind. Well, the floodgates opened. I told her all about the administration's latest series of unattainable goals and ridiculous methods and everything else that makes a teacher's world difficult at times. When I had finally gotten everything off my mind, I realized my wife was holding my hand. She waited patiently for me to quit whining and for me to lock eyes with her. Then, she squeezed my hand and said, "Aw, babe. This too shall pass." It felt so good to hear these words coming from another woman of God that had been placed in my life. I sprang up from my seat at the table and hugged my wife out of pure gratitude.

There is more truth in these four words than most of us realize. This world with all its heartache, hardships, despair, loss and grief is not what we were created for.

"This too shall pass"

-Mamaw Gert

September 21, 1905 – October 10, 1995

Watch Your Eyes

Every time my father would navigate his aluminum boat near a cypress limb to hang a yo-yo (aka Auto-fisher) or gun the motor to enter into a brushy duck blind, he would always shout out his usual preliminary warning, "Watch your eyes!" to whoever was in the front of the boat. My two older brothers and I always found this statement humorous. Not only is it physically impossible to watch your own eyes, but we would usually respond with some witty quip like "Why? Are they going to do tricks or something?" Now, of course, his true intention was to protect our optics from limbs and debris. So, after one such announcement, I inquired of him, "Why don't you say 'Cover your eyes,' or least something that is humanly possible?" I can still see him sitting in the back of that boat, hand on the tiller handle of the motor as he shook his head and responded, "Son, I don't know. Just habit, I guess."

Now days, my father is a grandfather to seven of the cutest kids God ever created and I'm blessed to call two of them mine. Today, I took one of my sons for a four-wheeler ride in our wooded property behind our house. When we came to a low-hanging limb wrapped in briars that had transversed our trail, I instinctively spoke over the engine and told my little boy, "Watch your eyes." After a few moments of contemplation, he twisted around to look up at me and said "Daddy, why you say that?" Looking down into those blue questioning eyes, I saw my father in the back of that old aluminum boat as I responded with an echo of his words, "Don't know, buddy. Just habit I guess."

And so it continues.

Sitting on My Sling

The bad luck I had endured from the previous deer season was obviously still lingering that next fall. I had entered the woods more than twenty times with either a bow or a gun and I had yet to even lay eyes on a deer. My bare freezer was a constant reminder of how drastic things were beginning to get.

I was beginning to accept my fate when, on a warm November morning, I saw a doe squirt across the pipeline like a brown lightning bolt. It happened so fast, I really didn't even have time to get excited. "Figures," I muttered to myself and I spent the majority of the uneventful morning staring at an empty pipeline. As a matter of fact, I sat there so long, my rear began to complain. I stood up, as much as a person can stand up in a box stand, and rearranged my metal folding chair and boat cushion. Once I was comfortable, I resumed guarding my food plot.

After a few moments, I noticed a doe standing in the line off to my left near the location where the doe had earlier sprinted across. This one was just standing there. Not feeding or particularly interested in anything. Just standing there as a broadside solution to my empty freezer conundrum.

"Welcome to my ice chest, little lady!" I whispered as I reached for my .270 propped in the corner. On its path to my shoulder, the gun abruptly stopped. Still looking at the deer, I tried again, this time with a bit more force. Once it reached a certain point, even though the gun was in mid-air, it refused to get any closer to my shoulder. I began to yank. Then, I noticed, with every yank, I was moving. I broke eye-contact with my target and looked down to see what exactly was taking place in this deer stand. I discovered that, during my furniture rearranging and completely unbeknownst to me, I had dead-centered the one-inch wide sling of my gun with the leg of my chair and I couldn't lift it because my body weight had it securely pinned to the floor of the stand.

As I desperately tried to free my sling, I slowly watched my backstraps disappear into the pines. By the time I was able to shoulder my rifle, the deer was gone. I was furious. I do believe that was the only time in my life I have ever gnawed on the stock of a firearm in order to maintain a Christian vocabulary. I threw my gun back to the corner and sank to a level of depression usually reserved for 6 year-olds who just dropped their ice cream cone.

Then, I heard it. A rustle that grew into a popping in the brush across the pipeline. Then, 60 yards away, out stepped the biggest, hairiest, nastiest (and several other –est's) buck I'd ever seen. He was intent on the doe that just made me look like a true knuckle-dragger and wasn't the least bit interested in me. With a chair-free sling, my gun found my shoulder and its bullet found its mark. I heard the shot. I heard the crash. I heard the angels sing. I found his 216-pound body, as well as the 140-class bone growth attached to his head, at the end of a 40-yard blood trail.

From this incident, I've learned that God's blessings truly do come in many forms, including keeping us from what we think we want in order to give us something better. However, I also learned that the Almighty has a scorching sense of humor.

Tall Tales

I have always enjoyed bass fishing in creeks and bayous. As I creep along in my small bass boat, I usually get the opportunity to watch wildlife, such as squirrels, turkeys and deer, along the banks. On one particular bass fishing trip, I noticed a small squirrel playing on the bank of the creek. He would scamper down a log that ran into the creek. He would make it almost to the water's edge and then retreat only to run down the log again. As I got closer, I saw what had the squirrel's attention. There was an acorn sitting on the log near the water. The squirrel would run almost to the acorn, then chicken out and withdraw. As I got closer, I checked on the progress of the squirrel's courage. I watched him run down the log and bravely tackle the acorn. As soon as his claws touched that acorn, a bass whose weight I would put not an ounce under 5 pounds, leapt out of the water and devoured the squirrel. I stood there with my jaw on my chest as it dawned upon me how timely I was to have seen this. If I hadn't been looking at that squirrel at that exact moment, I would have missed the whole once-in-a-lifetime spectacle. As I prepared to fish on, I heard a commotion in the water. I whipped my head around and there was that bass pushing that acorn back up on the log with his nose.

Another time, a buddy and I were running a trotline in the shallow flats of Black Lake. I could tell we had a nice one somewhere near the end by the tension and movement of the line. As we approached the fish, it shot for the bottom with impressive force. Finally, we decided I should stand up and attempt to hoist the line above my head, figuring the fish would have to surface once we took roughly 8 feet of slack out of the line. When I went for the pull, the line snapped. Frustrated, I threw the trotline back into the water. Then, I noticed movement in the water. Upon closer examination, I saw that, even though the fish had broken off, it never left. I whispered to my buddy to hand me the net as we might land this dumb fish after all. When the net touched the water, that fish took off like a bullet. Only he didn't head down. With his back barely under the water, he was headed right for a shallow bank. My buddy and I watched as this fish basically beached himself. "That was easy!" my buddy smirked as we went to retrieve the trapped fish. When we were about thirty yards away, the fish stood up and ran to the trees. In disbelief, I spun around to look at my buddy to see if he saw what I was pretty sure I did. With his mouth agape, he gunned the motor. When we had beached the boat, I grabbed the spotlight and began to search the trees. Movement caught my eye. "There!" I cried. When the light hit the creature, it climbed the tree it had been hiding behind. Determined to see what we were up against, I grabbed a spotlight and my buddy grabbed his pistol. The plan was pretty simple. "When I get this light on it, you introduce it to Jesus personally!" His pistol was raised as he took a nervous breath. But, when I flipped the on the light and shined up in the tree, the creature flew off.

Let me ask you a question. Have you ever heard a tall tale? Well, even if you haven't before, you have now. When we re-tell a tall tale, we usually make it personal as though the exaggerated events actually happened to us. We do this because personal stories are more exciting and believable because we were there and we have the opportunity to add detail to the already embellished story. As much as I love telling stories and entertaining, there is one story that I believe I tend to neglect and that would be my testimony of how Jesus Christ became my Savior. I refuse to believe I am alone in this predicament.

Good stories, like our testimonies, always have a relatable central character that undergoes some type of change. Boring stories would resemble a linear history lesson. For example, imagine if you came to me interested in what Christ has done in my life and I began that conversation by reading Genesis 1:1. Chances are you wouldn't be awake by the time I hit Deuteronomy. While I do believe that history is first among the curricula according to importance, to capture your attention I must make it relevant to you and illustrate how it is important to your current life.

One of the best known testimonies in the Word is found in the ninth chapter of the book of Acts. Here we see a rather determined individual named Saul who was taking a road trip with the sole purpose of causing pain. It was while he was on this journey that he met Christ in a rather unusual manner. A Heavenly-bright light, a booming voice that drove his face in the dirt, temporary blindness, an awkward conversation and precise directions all are found in this story of conversion. It is an awesome, powerful testimony.

Because of this splendid story, I often found myself hesitant to share my own testimony. Mine didn't have bright lights or booming voices. You see, before I was a Christian I went to church every Sunday. Before I came to know Christ, I read my Bible every day. I had the privilege of being raised by Christian parents who did not send me to church. They took me to church. Therefore, I knew who Jesus was before I knew Christ as my savior. So for me, it was as though I had opened a door and walked into the Christian part of my life. When I became old enough to realize my need for him, I accepted him and that was that.

Pretty boring, right? At least that's what I thought for many years. But then I came to realize that a testimony is an opportunity to tell others what God did for you. It doesn't have to be a tall tale meant to impress or even some unrelated history lesson. It does, however, need to be a highly personalized story about what God means to you and how Jesus changed your life. So, the lesson I learned is this: Don't worry. There is no such thing as a "bad" testimony. Even though the outcome for every believer is the same, no two paths are the same. Besides, if I wanted to tell you about God's provisions and love for me, it would come from a different point in my walk with Christ.

I was in my last summer of college. Foolishly, I had bragged that I was going to spend that summer playing softball on the weekends, bass fishing in the evenings and going to class when absolutely necessary. Well, God had other plans. A ruptured disc in my back put my ball playing on hiatus. God had removed that sport, which was fun but not really beneficial in any way, from my life and I was upset. Then, a conversation with a young lady in my class led to a date that following weekend. Conveniently, I was not playing ball and had ample time on my hands during the weekends. That date eventually led to an engagement 6 months later. I didn't play ball because of my injury, I never touched the water that summer because I was too busy spending time with my love and I rarely missed class because that would have been a missed opportunity to see her. God took what I thought I wanted and replaced it with a much greater blessing. That blessing has now given birth to two more blessings in the forms of our sons, Reagan and Michael. Now, that is a testimony I will share without hesitation or invitation.

In the 21st chapter of his gospel, John refers to his works as his testimony (v. 24). When we look at it, that's exactly what all four of the gospels are—testimonies of witnesses. They tell us how these four men, from very different backgrounds, perceived, interacted, learned from and were changed by Christ. They also give us the only documentation of Jesus as he walked this earth. Imagine if they had neglected to share them. Imagine the greatest story ever told not being passed on. These thoughts beg the question, "with whom do you need to share yours?"

Forget about impressing others. Just share how you were changed or how you are still being transformed into a new creation. Others need to hear it. As Paul encouraged young Timothy, so I urge you, *"Do not be ashamed to testify about our Lord."* (2 Tim. 1:8).

Why I Hunt

In today's culture, hunting animals seems to have several negative denotations trailing it about. The idea of killing one's own table fare is repulsive to some. I can even recall reading an article where some dear soul had written in to chastise hunters for being so cruel. This concerned citizen even went so far as to offer hunters the advice of abandoning their barbaric practices of killing defenseless animals and purchasing their meat at the supermarket where no animals had to be killed. While I'm in no way assuming all anti-hunters fall into this person's IQ range, I do applaud this intellectual and his or her sound doctrine and wish them and their death-free meat all the best. However, I feel an explanation to the masses of the sport of deer hunting might be in order.

Let me begin by saying that the actual harvesting of the animal is the most un-fun part of hunting. That is not to say I do not enjoy a successful hunt. It's just at that point, the real work begins. By work, I mean the dragging, hanging, cleaning and dressing of the deer. If everybody loved getting their hands bloody, deer processors and butcher shops would soon be out of business. No, the real fun for me begins in the summer.

My boys ride along as we clear shooting lanes and hang feeders. They ask how big will the deer be that this particular stand produces and how many "deer nuggets" (a.k.a. fried deer steak) it will render. The fun is showing my boys how we manage our land to provide cover, browse and sanctuary for the deer. The fun is checking trail cameras and showing the boys what creatures we share our land with. The fun is teaching them to examine the forest floor for tracks and allowing them to determine the species.

The fun is packing our bags with the bare essentials, (i.e. an extra flashlight and skinning knife, a Bible, snacks, word-search books for my little ones, etc.) and seeing the joy in my older son's eyes when he is presented with his very own bag complete with all the accessories.

The fun is the opportunity a box stand offers on a cool drizzly morning to spend time with the Maker and his Word. The fun is watching a sun rise through the hardwood of a creek bottom as it displays colors that no adjective in the English language could adequately describe. The fun part is witnessing the blaze of colors the occasional gum and maple produce beneath the pine canopy during the fall, whose colors are only surpassed by the snowy dogwoods of spring. The fun is listening to the eerie wail of the wood ducks as they roost in a nearby beaver pond or of searching the skies for the southern-bound geese that produce the tale-tell, raspy honk. The fun is watching a frisky cat squirrel and his twin chase each other up and down a white oak near my stand. The fun is walking up on a spot of freshly pawed earth or discovering a sapling recently removed of its bark and explaining its meaning and purpose to my little ones.

The fun is the tap on my leg as my son points and excitedly whispers with eyes the size of saucers, "Daddy, a deer! I think its a buck." The fun is telling and re-telling of how it all happened to your friends and brothers at the skinning shed.

The fun is processing the animal while hopefully teaching my son a lot more than just what a backstrap looks like. The fun is sitting at the dining room table with my family as we ask the Father's blessing over a meal of venison, creamed corn, purple-hull peas, and potatoes all of which were harvested on our hill.

The fun part is dreaming up new shooting lanes, scoping out areas of high deer traffic as future stand spots and giving my children the chance to name these spots they will one day inherit.

So, why do I do it? Why do I repeatedly leave a toasty bed at insane a.m. hours? Why do I labor tirelessly all year for a season lasting a couple of months? Why do I record movement shown on my trail cameras and compare those with moon phases, weather forecasts and projected prime feeding times? Why, even with a tired body and addled brain, do I look with giddy anticipation for our next chance to know what a rain-soaked climbing stand smells like? Why do I hunt? Well, because it's fun.

What are you leaving behind?

O pening day of deer season is a sacred time with my family. We meet with the entire family at my father's house. With ATVs and side x sides parked outside, we discuss who is going where over coffee and biscuits. One such morning, as I was loading up my four-wheeler, my father called me over to his truck. He handed me a rolled down, less-than-a-third full bag of deer corn. "Put this out in the grass patch on the way to your stand." "Yes, sir." I responded as I put the bag on my back rack. Then, he handed me another identical bag. "Run this over to your brother's house and tell him to do the same." Again, I took it and secured to the back of my Honda.

Upon reaching my brother's house, I met him coming down his front porch steps. I parked near his ATV and waited for him. When he got there, I handed him the bag of deer corn and repeated our father's instructions, "Here, put this in your stand's grass patch." Then, the complaining began. "Seriously? I've got farther to drive than everybody else. I'm not going to have time. If I go to the patch, I'll have to walk past my stand. Besides, we've got those automatic feeders that do this for us now. I mean.…. Why do I have to do it?" It struck me as odd. Here I was with my brother. We are both grown, college-educated men with wives, families and mortgages and he really just asked me "Why do I have to do it?" To which my response was "Because Daddy said so!" "Oh, OK," he said as he took the bag and departed. The fact that our father gave the order ended the discussion, even though the discussion was between two grown men.

We all know that we affect those who come after us. But do

we ever consider to what extent? Would it be totally audacious of us as mere mortals to believe that our influence could reach 10 years into the future? 100 years? I mean, how long can we expect our actions to linger?

In order to answer this question, we must first realize that strong families survive from one generation to the next because of the diligence applied to the teaching process. I believe that instruction weaves very comfortably, very naturally into the fabric of everyday life. In other words, teaching is going to happen. In that, we have no say. However, the kind of teaching, whether it be good or bad, is entirely left up to us.

Let's examine the two, shall we? I'll begin with good and what the Word has to say on the topic. Let's first look at Deuteronomy 7:9, which tells us *"Know therefore that the Lord your God is God; he is the faithful God, keeping his covenant of love to a thousand generations of those who love him and keep his commands."* Here we find a promise, not of a hundred years or even a thousand years, but of a thousand generations of those who love and seek the Lord.

This same promise of a thousand generations shows up again in Exodus 20:5b-6 where God says, *"For I, the Lord your God, am a jealous God, punishing the children for the sin of the fathers to the third and fourth generation of those who hate me, but showing love to a thousand {generations} of those who love me and keep my commandments."* While this promise is awesome, do we consider what the 20th chapter of Exodus houses? This is where we find the Ten Commandments. If we believe the Ten Commandments to still be valid, then we must trust the promise found within them.

God kicks this whole "love to a thousand generations" up a notch using the words found in verses seventeen and eighteen of the 103rd Psalm. *"But from everlasting to everlasting the Lord's love is with those who fear him, and his righteousness with their children's children- with those who keep his covenant and remember to obey his precepts.*" As if thousands of generations of blessings weren't impressive enough, our Lord shows us we haven't seen anything yet by dwarfing those promises with "everlasting to everlasting."

Now, let's take a look at what happens to those who teach evil. I believe that Jeremiah 32:18 sums up this lifestyle best when it says "*You show love to thousands but bring the punishment for the fathers' sins into the laps of their children after them.*" What this passage is saying is that if the father is a thief, alcoholic or drug dealer, then the children will have to deal with that sin. It could be that, due to a childhood saturated with it, they may pick up the habit itself. It could be having to live with the name recognition. As we all know, especially in the South, one of the first questions to come out of a father's mouth to a young man wishing to court his daughter is "Who's your daddy, son?" This verse in no way means that a sinner's child is automatically doomed to hell. If that were the case, Heaven would be one empty joint. It does, however, mean that the child must confront that sin.

As I said before, we teach our children. There is simply no way around it. My father taught me to love and appreciate hunting and fishing. My mother instilled in me a passion to teach. These are things that I cherish and I plan on passing down to my children. However, I have found that when we, as mere mortals, lead our children to trust in Christ, we touch eternity.

So, let's ask ourselves, what are we leaving behind? Has our life been one of love and devotion that would bless our descendents? Will God use you to bless the generations to come? How will our life affect those family members we've yet to meet?

The Most Beautiful Evening I Never Saw

ᴍ

Campfires and I just seem to go together well. Black Lake and I have been close friends for years. So, as you can imagine, fires on the banks of Black Lake are my area of expertise. It is here I do my best work. By "work" I mean relaxing and enjoying life. When a fire is built, it isn't long before a crowd of family members begins to congregate. Orange faces encircle the blaze while marshmallows are roasted and stories are re-told. While these moments are cherished and I'm sure I'll look back on these gatherings with misty eyes, it's the aftermath of such get-togethers that I covet. When the crowd and fire both die down, I find myself alone with the embers. Watching the coals shimmer as the occasional flame bursts forth is one of life's simple pleasures for me. In the quiet warmth of the glow, I have the occasion to converse with the Almighty. Some of my most comforting talks and revealing answers to prayers have occurred at times such as these. None, however, could rival this past winter.

The fire was built, family arrived and a grand time was had by all. Then, after a spell, the elders of the crowd slapped their knees, and while rising from their seat announced it was past their bedtime while the mothers herded their little ones toward their bathtubs. Before long, I found myself alone by the fire. Now, without going into great detail, I have a rare condition that forces my eyelids closed (more on that in "A Look At Life Through Closed Eyes"). So basically, I sat there, blindly wondering if I would ever be able to enjoy the splendor of a fire without propping my eyelids open and pretty much feeling sorry

59

for myself. Then, I heard it. For quite possibly the first time, I truly heard the voice of the fire. The chorus of pops, hisses and cracks was soon accompanied by other previously-unnoticed sounds. The peeping of the poule-d'eaus feeding in the grassy shallow water was perceived just before the gentle lapping of the waves against the dock. Then, I noticed the birds of the day were not yet conceding to their nocturnal counterparts. As I sat there enjoying this unusual symphony, I noticed that the quietness also afforded me the opportunity to hear the wind chimes on my mother's front porch as they swayed in the pleasing breeze better than two hundred yards away. The icing on the acoustic cake came in the form of a mallard hen. Rafted up somewhere out on the placid lake, she called to her companions with a crescendo of raspy quacks. This evening was, in a word, beautiful and it's beauty was only enhanced by my handicap.

Then, I began to ponder, "How many of these audio-delightful evenings had I missed because I was simply too busy looking? How many times had I let things that I deemed important keep me from the greater things that God had in store? How many blessings have I missed out on because I didn't follow the ridiculously simple directions found in the tenth verse of the 46th Psalm which says, *"Be still and know that I am God."*?

From now on I'm looking forward to enjoying so much more than just a campfire.

A Look at Life Through Closed Eyes

Blepharospasms. This funny-sounding word, which meant nothing to me up until the spring of 2013, has now taken a front row seat in my life. The medical field defines it as "derived from the Greek word 'blepharo' meaning eyelid, it is an uncontrollable abnormal contraction of the eyelids, which if chronic, can cause lifelong challenges. In rare cases, the symptoms result in functional blindness. The subject's eyelids feel like they are clamping shut and will not open without great effort or the physical use of one's fingers. Patients may have 20/20 vision but for long periods of time are effectively blind." I describe it as imagine having a big picture window with the blinds closed.

It began when I noticed that on my daily commute to pick up our oldest son, 5-year-old Reagan, from school, I felt like I was getting sleepy and my eyes wanted to shut. I soon began dreading driving long distances. Light also seemed to hurt my eyes more than usual. This led to an appointment with an optometrist, which led to an appointment with an ophthalmologist, who referred me to a neuro-opthamologist, which led me to neurologists in Shreveport and Houston who decided upon blepharospasms as my diagnosis. According to my research this relatively-rare, incurable condition affects one out of every twenty thousand Americans and the lot of fate fell to me.

My life has been significantly changed since my diagnosis. I saw my passion for teaching in the public school system come to an abrupt halt as I was first placed on extended sick leave and am now staring down a disability retirement at the ripe old age of 33. I have also been deprived of my ability to drive. Summer day trips to my wife's office to surprise her with a lunch date, picking up my son from school and getting to hear about his day's activities, helping coach his ball games, loading up my family and pulling the bass boat to the lake for a relaxing weekend all became things of the past in a matter of months.

I now truly understand Jesus' words in John 21:18, *"I'm telling you the very truth now: When you were young you dressed yourself and went wherever you wished, but when you get old you'll have to stretch out your hands while someone else dresses you and takes you where you don't want to go."* My son has essentially become my eyes. I clutch his hand and through a series of movements he is able to lead me through parking lots, up and down stairs, and around brightly-lit (and usually spasm-inducing) super markets. His aunt is his first grade teacher. One evening she couldn't wait to tell me about the day's lesson. The topic was animals and how they help people. A mule can pull a wagon and a cow supplies milk, etc. Then, she discussed how some animals help handicapped people. After she had illustrated the job description of a seeing-eye dog, Reagan's hand shot up as he exclaimed, "I do that for my Daddy!" So from that point on, I've had my own seeing-eye Reagan.

Now, it would be easy to dwell on and complain of all which this condition has deprived me. However, I must admit, it has also granted me a few things. For one, I was always uncomfortable being a school teacher and a youth minister to the same group of kids. One requires a professional distance and discipline whereas the other offers a much more personal approach. I had discovered that the children had a difficult time differentiating between Mr. Dupree, the assistant principal who had to uphold the punishment for cell phone use on campus, and Mr. Ben who was texting them about a pizza party and Bible study at his house that evening. However, due to my condition, that has been one less worry on my mind. I've been able to commit myself fully to my ministry and maintain contact with most of my beloved students.

Due to the amount of time I can now direct towards the youth group, I've seen our numbers swell and I still get the opportunity to teach. I also have had time to pick up another passion that I had allowed to slip between the cracks of everyday life and that is my writing. Looking at computer screens seems to disagree with me now, so this work and most others were originally recorded on loose leaf paper with a fountain pen probably in a deer stand. Speaking of deer stands, there are some things in my life that I refuse to give up, no matter what my condition may be and one of those is my time in a deer stand.

Several people have asked me how it is possible for a person with my condition to deer hunt. I believe my father answered that inquiry best when he said, "It could be just like me when I read a book in the stand. Every once in a while, I look up. Every once in a while, you could lift an eyelid and glance around." While the proof that method obviously works for him hangs over his recliner in the form of a 160-class rack, I've found other methods to be useful. First off, I try to hunt in hardwood creek bottoms or ridges. Hunting here in these close-quarter situations allows me to hear the deer approaching. If I'm hunting a pipeline stand or one with a long shooting lane, then my "seeing-eye Reagan" comes into play.

It was quite a thrill to feel that tap on my leg followed by a whispered "Daddy, a deer. I think it's a buck." He enjoys re-telling that story over a plate of fried backstrap or "deer nuggets" as they are known around our house. Not only does my condition make hunting more difficult, but getting to the stand has also become a challenge. Most of the trees along the trails on my property bear 4-wheeler rack-high scars thanks to untimely spasms. Even when walking, I must pause frequently and wait for my eyes to re-open. Enough about me, the condition and my life with it. On to the story.

One misty morning, I walked to a stand that's only a few hundred yards from my back door. As I navigated my way through the tunnel of briars and underbrush, I had a spasm. I stopped, took a deep breath and lowered my head. At that second, a single drop of water grew large enough to break away from the limb that collected it and found its way to the back of my unprotected neck. As that chilly little moist sphere made its way down my spine, I ridiculed my luck. Of all the places to have a spasm, of all the places to stop, of all the places on my body to leave uncovered. Just as quick, another thought, or memory I should say, jumped into my mind. The word "luck" must have triggered it. I could vividly recall sharing a bass boat with a friend, Jeremy Riggs, and the topic of our luck came up. On that trip he told me his grandfather's/ preacher's outlook on the subject. He said he believes there is no such thing as luck--only God's blessings. At that moment, even though the spasm had passed, I remained motionless. I listened as the Almighty spoke to me through that drop.

"Do you really think your condition caught me by surprise? My child, just has I needed you to be in that exact spot for the single drop of water to touch your only swatch of uncovered skin, so you are exactly where I need you to be at this phase of your life." Then the grandfather's perception made more sense than ever. There is no such thing as luck, whether we perceive it as good or bad. In reality, it is all God's blessing. I'm reminded of Paul and his thorn and God's answer to his predicament. *"My grace is sufficient for you and my power is made perfect in weakness."* 2 Corinthians 12:9.

I'll admit to you my fear of the unknown. I don't know where this will lead or how my family and I will fare through it all. But I serve a God who does know and loves me enough to even have a plan for it. So, instead of viewing my condition as a handicap and focus on the negatives like losing my public school classroom or being robbed of my ability to go wherever I want, whenever I want, I will look with giddy anticipation to how God plans to use me in the future. But, I will also long for that day when I will gaze upon the face of my Savior with eyes that don't know how to spasm. Until then, I will echo John's words found at the Bible's conclusion, *"Amen, come Lord Jesus."*

Although I'm sure I will stumble and fall back into self pity as Satan reminds me of my weaknesses from time to time, I am determined to view my time here on earth, all of it, not as a circumstance of bad luck, but rather a blessing given with a purpose in mind. That will be my outlook on life, even if it is through closed eyes.

A Dying Way of Life

R emember a time when your GPS and fish finder were rolled into one trusty device known as a Papaw? Remember when your weather forecast was your grandmother's glance to the sky? I certainly can. However, I don't have to jump a generation to find those that possess such powers. I can recall sitting on my parents' front porch with my best friend, Ryan Stewart, discussing our plans to go "grabbing" (aka "noodling." aka "run your hand down in a submerged hole and wait for a territorial catfish to attack it and then drag him out." If this sport was not birthed by bored rednecks, I'm not sitting here.) My father emerged from his house, paused on his porch long enough to hear of our plan, stared at a partly cloudy sky and then matter-of-factly stated, "Boys, yall had better hurry. It's gonna rain in about an hour." Then he walked off the porch and meandered out of sight. Ryan turned to me, "How does he know that? He didn't say 'It looks like rain' or 'It might rain'. He said it's gonna rain! And you know what? I believe it's going to rain… within the hour! Why? Because Roy Dupree said so!" Thirty minutes later, a distant sound of thunder. An hour later, a deluge.

How did they do it? How did Papaw know where the deer that were being chased by our hounds were going to cross that old logging road? How did Daddy know what color bait would work best on that particular body of water on that particular day? How did he know what tree to throw by and even call the exact moment when the fish would latch on? How did he know when to expect the bluegills to bed or the trotline catfish to survive the night? How did Mamaw make her sweet pickles or Mama make her duck and dressing without ever glancing at a recipe? I can recall asking Daddy how he knew exactly when to plant the purple hull peas or the G-90 sweet corn we grow on our hill. His reply was "It's just time." I was always baffled by how, on a bass fishing trip down on Saline creek, my father could just strike out through the seemingly unending and repetitious swamp and always end up at the exact fork where he had intended to begin fishing. No compass. No GPS. He didn't even follow the twisty creek. He just went. Don't even get me started on his bass fishing itself. I could throw in a spot twice and as I was leaving, he would walk up behind me and toss in the exact same hole. "I already threw there, Daddy." "Um-huh" came his undeterred reply. Seconds later he was dragging a bass up on the bank. After he attached that fish to his stringer, he'd throw in the same spot again with strikingly similar success. I've seen him catch upwards of four bass from behind the same cypress. Occurrences such as these led my brothers and me to give him the nickname "The Fish Whisperer." We would often state that if Roy was in the fishing party, everybody else was competing for second place.

One day, as I grew frustrated with how he just "knew" to do things, I exclaimed, "Daddy, I can't do half the stuff you can. By the time I have children, they won't know how to do anything!" "Just watch," was his only reply. There's a lot of truth in those two words. Truth that sadly I didn't fully notice until my grandparents had already left this earth. But, as I watched my parents, slowly I began to perceive and, more importantly, record the manner, time of year and frequency of how certain things were done. I write in a journal everyday simply because my father records his daily activities in a planner. I grow a garden and process and preserve the vegetables because my mother taught me how. Slowly but surely, I'm learning. Learning how to create certain dishes, blanch and put up peas and corn, when to spray certain fruit trees and when the catfish start biting on trotlines again. I was not born with this knowledge. While I believe that teaching weaves very naturally into everyday life, it does require a willing student. Your children are not going to need you to teach them to use the latest technology gadget. They will magically manage that feat on their own. However, the things of your past that you treasure will require some instruction if they are to take root in the next generation. Your children will need you to teach them what you've learned.

How many times do we wistfully state, "I sure do wish things were like they used to be" or "I wish I could taste her cooking just once" or "If I could clean fish with him just one more time"? We can remember, so why can't we re-create? Could it be that when the opportunity was laid before us, we were too busy with things, hobbies, and jobs that we thought were important? Judge the worth of these activities by this simple question: Do you hope your children learn to benefit from them?

So please, for the sake of the next generation, sit down, quit being so busy and learn from the elders before it's too late. Don't let their knowledge, methods and stories die with them. Take the time to learn about how and why they did things in their everyday lives. Even if it requires you to take a day or two off from your vocation, I believe the benefits will far outweigh the cost. Sit down with your grandmother and learn how to can garden vegetables and venison like they did when they didn't have the luxury of a freezer. Watch her make her wonderful chicken and dressing and try to duplicate it right along beside her. Tag along the next time your father brings his beagles or squirrel dog into the woods and see what lessons await you. Shut up and listen to your uncle and his tales of his raccoon-hunting days. If you don't have the opportunity to do these things because of where you live or these treasured individuals are already gone, then just read this book.

While not a complete "how-to" manual on life, in my meager opinion, it will provide a glimpse of days gone by.

But above all, record your own lessons. Write these, not only for the sake of your feeble memory, but also for the sake of those who come after you. The items that I do possess that are hand-written by my grandparents (stories, records, and even the minutes of a family meeting called after their father's death, etc.) are among some of my most cherished belongings. Also, in addition to my daily journal, I also keep a binder whose title page reads "Everything you need to know and don't need to forget." It contains directions on how to make my grandmother's pound cake and my mother's mayhaw jelly. It contains step-by-step directions of how my father makes his famous fried Black Lake catfish and an elderly deacon's detailed directions on how to create and operate your very own smokehouse (It's easier than you may think). It has our family tree all the way back to my great, great, great-grandfather John Dupree, whom we refer to as "The Reverend," who started practically every Baptist church in this area. It contains a photograph of my great-grandfather and great-grandmother on their wedding day, December 22, 1898.

During a recent conversation with my brother Dan, I realized that he takes the preservation of such memories even a step farther. He said that at family get-togethers when everybody starts breaking out the video cameras, he always tries to focus on the faces more than the events. He will try to zoom in on every face in the room. I believe that footage will one day come in handy when the future family members want to know more about those who have already passed on. It will give the youngsters an opportunity to view their elders at a point in time when their ages would have been roughly the same and allow them to see which member of the family they most resemble physically.

Things change so fast. In my short 33 years upon this earth,

I've witnessed everyday household items become a thing of the past. I grew up with a wood-burning fireplace as my source of warmth during the winter. Now I use central heat. I have seen cell phones go from props in sci-fi movies to chunky bag phones that were about as portable as a brick to modern touch-screen devices with seemingly limitless features that can fit in your pocket. I've witnessed the surrender of the 8-track (of which I still own many) to the blurred years of cassettes and compact discs to now the readily downloadable MP3 files.

Things change and they do it quickly. People leave this world and they often do it without warning. Don't let the past die with its generation. Don't let your way of doing things become *A Dying Way of Life*.

For Ryan

"May our kind never pass from this earth."

P.S.

Thank you for traveling this path with me. I hope you enjoyed reading the stories and lessons as much as I did writing them. However, if at this book's conclusion you are merely entertained, I have failed. I hope I have challenged you to look at your own ever-changing life and decide what may be worth jotting down for others to learn from and enjoy. But even above that, I hope I have urged you to either enrich or begin your walk with Christ. Either way, rest assured you have been prayed for. I thank God for you taking the time to read my work and I ask him to speak to you through it.

God bless,

Ben Dupree

CPSIA information can be obtained
at www.ICGtesting.com
Printed in the USA
FFOW02n2017280415
13028FF